N'Heures Souris Rames

The Coucy Castle Manuscript

Coucy Castle: a late nineteenth-century view of the ruins.

N'Heures Souris Rames

The Coucy Castle Manuscript

Translated & Annotated by
Ormonde de Kay

Clarkson N. Potter, Inc., Publishers
Distributed by Crown Publishers, Inc., New York

Inquiries should be addressed to Clarkson N. Potter, Inc., One Park Avenue, New York, New York 10016

Printed in the United States of America

Published simultaneously in Canada by General Publishing Company Limited

Library of Congress Cataloging in Publication Data

de Kay, Ormonde, 1923-
    N'Heures Souris Rames: The Coucy Castle Manuscript

    Forty homophonic French verses that read as English Mother Goose rhymes.
    Bibliography
    Includes index.
        1. Macaronic literature.   2. Nonsense-verses.   3. Nursery rhymes—Anecdotes, facetiae, satire, etc.   4. Parodies.   I. Mother Goose.   II. Title.
PN1489.Z7D4   1980   841   80-16043
ISBN 0-517-540819

10 9 8 7 6 5 4 3 2 1

First Edition

To the memory
of
Luis d'Antin van Rooten
and
a dear friend who loved words,
Michael Anthony George Knibbs

Salus men grandi
Boigne non mansdet.
Cris ce nom tout citet
Marie dons ouai ne ce dist.
Tu qui l'entoures ce teis
Ourson feraulles dist ~
D'aul dans sauntistet
Beurret dans sauntet.
Decesse dinne
D'uefs cales o men grandi.

A verse from the original manuscript.

Preface

IT WAS WITH CONSIDERABLE CURIOSITY but no presentiment of what lay ahead that, on returning to my study from my front door one morning and seating myself at my desk, I slit open the bulky manila envelope that had arrived in the mail and drew forth from between cardboard stiffeners a thick sheaf of photostats. Each showed a page inscribed, in what I would eventually come to know as the *bâtarde* hand, with short passages of verse in archaic French. These, then, were the copies of his remarkable manuscript, the *N'Heures Souris Rames*, the Collector had said he would send me. Pushing the galleys on my desk to one side and laying out half a dozen of the photostats in their place, I recalled how the verses had come my way.

At that time, early in June of 1977, I had for five months been the modestly paid editor (and staff) of *Manuscripts,* the quarterly journal of the Manuscript Society, and in that capacity had only a week or so before attended the society's annual four-day convention, held, that year, in Los Angeles. Among the fifty-odd members and spouses present was a lean, dark-haired man in his middle years, with heavy-lidded eyes and an imperious beak nose, who seemed very much out of place; whereas everyone else had, on arriving, decked himself out in colorful casual attire, he never failed to wear a sober suit and tie, and while the others hobnobbed happily throughout the long bus rides between "events," he barricaded himself behind his *New York Times* or some book. One evening, coming upon him alone at a table in the Century Plaza cocktail lounge, I yielded to an impulse to introduce myself. After an awkward moment he coldly asked me, in an accent I couldn't place, what I collected; I replied that I knew nothing about manuscripts, having been hired to edit the society journal on the basis of previous editorial jobs. My answer surprised him but evidently didn't displease him: staring at me intently, he began to ply me with further questions. On learning that I was a writer and occasional poet, knew French, and had some notion of European history, he grew increasingly cordial, and at last invited me to join him.

Over drinks, my new acquaintance talked freely about himself. Hungarian by birth and upbringing, he was in the import-export business and a collector of manuscript verses from the era of the Renaissance and earlier. He had joined the Society and come to its convention hoping to find a purchaser for a rare sixteenth-century manuscript, but had learned to his chagrin, on consulting the list of participating members and their specialties, that not one of these people qualified even remotely as a prospect. He was enjoying the convention program, notably the visit to the Huntington Library, with its priceless old manuscripts, and, for fun, the tour of the Universal lot, but he had no wish to consort with collectors of Civil War letters and Western Americana, let alone collectors of autographs of movie stars, aviators, sports figures, nightclub entertainers, and convicted murderers. (No doubt about it, he was a snob, a manuscripts snob, and another valued new acquaintance, the dealer Charles Hamilton, would, I knew, despise him for it; nevertheless, in view of the enormous pleasure he has brought me, I cannot, with a good conscience, condemn him.)

The Hungarian businessman and I were often in each other's company after that, and on the last night of the convention, following the annual banquet in a Bel Air Hotel dining room, the Collector (as I now thought of him) came over to my table and pulled up a chair. With deliberation, he unwrapped a cigar and lighted it, studying me from under those drooping lids. Had I ever heard of a village in Picardy called Caix? he asked me abruptly, spelling out the word. I told him my grandfather believed our family had originated there and that the spelling of our name had changed to de Kay in Holland, whither some ancestor had fled from the late-sixteenth-century religious wars convulsing France. Had I heard of Coucy Castle? Of course, I said, it was a famous old medieval fortress about forty miles from Caix. The Collector seemed satisfied; glancing around to make sure he could not be overheard, he leaned closer, and in a guarded voice related a curious tale. The manuscript he was trying to sell, he said, had been found in the rubble of Coucy Castle in 1917, after German bombardments and, later, blasting had demolished the old structure, and had been acquired by an American collector from whose heirs the Collector had bought it. He had subsequently learned, however, that the manuscript was not his but the French Government's, inasmuch as Coucy Castle had been state property since 1856. So he dared not advertise it for sale or put it up for auction. He would continue to hunt quietly for a buyer, but in the meantime, if I were interested, he would furnish me with a copy, provided I gave him my word not to show it or even mention its existence to anyone.

Visions of becoming embroiled in an international lawsuit made me hesitate, but then I reflected that reading old French verses was hardly a criminal act; I agreed to the Collector's terms, and we shook on it. On returning to New York I looked up Coucy Castle in sundry encyclopedias. I learned that some of the twelfth-century lords of Coucy had been notorious brigands, and one, Gui II, a troubadour. I read about their celebrated device: *Roy ne suis, ne prince, ne duc, ne comte aussy, je suis sire de Coucy* ("I am neither king, nor prince, nor duke, nor count either, I am the sire of Coucy"). And I learned that the castle, sold to Louis de France, duc d'Orléans, in 1400 and passing to the French crown on the accession of Louis XII in 1498, had been an appanage of Claude de France (later François I's queen) and of Diane de France during the sixteenth century, when someone, presumably someone on the premises, had compiled the mysterious verses.

On glancing through my copies of those verses I was jolted by a sense of *déjà lu:* they seemed eerily familiar, echoes from my remote childhood. Odd, I thought, that the Collector hadn't mentioned this—until I realized that, growing up in Hungary, he would have absorbed an entirely different set of spoken and written sounds. But the verses also reminded me, insistently, of those in one of my favorite books, Luis d'Antin van Rooten's *Mots d'Heures: Gousses, Rames.* Reaching for my copy, I turned to the foreword: "The most fascinating quality of these verses," van Rooten had written therein, "is to be found upon reading them aloud in the sonorous, measured classic style made famous by the Comédie Française at the turn of the century . . . ; these poems then assume a strangely familiar, almost nostalgic, homely quality." Exactly! What van Rooten had observed anent the d'Antin Manuscript applied equally, I saw, to the Coucy Castle Manuscript.

In puzzling out the title of the old verses he had received in manuscript as the bequest of a Provençal kinsman, van Rooten had translated *Mots d'Heures: Gousses, Rames* as "Words of the Hours: Root and Branch." But what was I to make of *N'Heures Souris Rames*, the title that, according to the Collector, covered the verses before me? "Not hours mouse [or mice] sticks [twigs, oars]"? It made no sense. I jotted down the two French titles on the back of an envelope and studied them. Noticing, first, that *heures* and *rames* occurred in both, I asked myself whether such a coincidence could be accidental, and decided it was unlikely. Next, looking up *souris* in my French-English dictionary, I discovered that in addition to signifying the well-known cheese-eating rodent, it was an archaic and poetic word for the noun "smile" (nowadays *sourire*), in both the singular and the plural. I was getting warmer, I felt, but I still didn't see how the two titles could be related. Then, in a flash, it came to me that some ingenious Picard scribe with time on his hands and a copy of the Provençal *Mots d'Heures* at hand could have been inspired to try his own hand, literally as well as figuratively, at the same game. In the light of this possibility, the title chosen by the author/compiler of the verses not only made sense but was eminently apposite: *Not Hours* (to distinguish them from their model, the *Words of the Hours*) *Smiles* (indicating that he sought to amuse) *Offshoots* (of the Provençal verses).*

The more deeply I delved in the *N'Heures Souris Rames* the more compelling I found them, and before long, in the grip of an

---

*A friend suggests the alternate reading *Off-Hours Smiles Reams*. "Off-hours" seems quite possible, but "reams" less so, since the sheets making up the manuscript number nowhere near five hundred, or even fifty. Incidentally, the scribe may have been idled, and so afforded time for versifying, by an innovation dating from the previous century: the printing press.

obsession much like the one Luis van Rooten must have known, I found myself, willy-nilly, striving to unriddle their many surface mysteries. With the example of my predecessor's broad learning, brilliant insights, and virtuoso leaps of creative scholarly imagination before me, I did my best to pierce the mists of the intervening centuries and determine the author's meanings, incidentally modernizing his Middle French spellings, as van Rooten had done with his manuscript, for sweet clarity's sake. And as the work progressed, what a vivid, many-sided picture of sixteenth-century French society emerged! I was struck by how often the name Anne appeared in the manuscript, and concluded, tentatively, that the poet was thereby making discreet bows to the memory of Louis XII's queen Anne de Bretagne, who, dying in 1514, would have been well remembered by her daughter Claude de France, chatelaine of Coucy until *her* death ten years later. Again, the frequent recurrence of certain nouns and verbs (e.g., in alphabetical order, *ail* [garlic], *âne* [donkey], *crailler* [to caw], *huile* [oil], *oie* [goose], *ouaille* [sheep], *ouate* [wadding], *paille* [straw], and *scier* [to saw]) could be explained by the fact that in the sixteenth century Picardy, and indeed all France, was still largely agricultural.

I naturally kept the Collector informed about my project, sending him batches of annotated verses from time to time; but having promised not to reveal the manuscript's existence, I dared not entertain the hope of ever presenting the fruits of my labors to the public. The reader can imagine my feelings, then, when, just as I was completing my self-appointed task, my correspondent informed me that he had sold the Coucy Castle Manuscript, in secret, to a collector who was ready to hide the papers, if need be, in a place where even the craftiest and most dedicated agents of Interpol and the French Sûreté could never find them. The new owner's identity was safe with the Collector, and since the French authorities, however eager they might be to repossess the old manuscript, could certainly not object to its contents being divulged in a scholarly monograph, I was free to do what I liked with my copies.

The result is this little book.

It remains for me to express my ardent gratitude to the Collector, whom I cannot, obviously, name. My thanks are due to Barry Morentz, a keen student of medieval and Renaissance calligraphy, who established the unknown scribe's *bâtarde* hand, and to Cathérine Dop of the N.Y.U. French Department, who solved occasional puzzles of Middle French (and specifically Picard) orthography. I also wish to apologize to my wife, Barbara, and son, Thomas, for neglecting them during the countless evening and weekend hours I spent immured in my study and immersed in my quest. Finally, with profound respect tinged with regret that I was never privileged to know him, I must acknowledge my incalculable debt to the late Luis d'Antin van Rooten, whose pioneering work in a previously overlooked field of French letters inspired me from the start.

ORMONDE DE KAY
New York City
April 1, 1980

N'Heures Souris Rames

The Coucy Castle Manuscript

Georgie Port-régie, peu digne en paille,
Qui se dégeule sans mais.[1] Dame craille.[2]
Où haine de bouées ce qu'aime a tout pilé:
Georgie Port-régie règne. Ohé![3]

This quatrain appears to contain a prophecy, like the quatrains making up the famous *Centuries* (Lyon, 1555) of the Provençal seer Nostradamus. The Georgian port control or port-controller may refer to Georgia in the Caucasus or Georgia in the United States. From the context, however, it seems more likely that *Georgie* is a jocular name for George Washington, leader of the upstart United States, who, as such, controls its ports; he is portrayed—two centuries or more before the world would become aware of him—as a rude bumpkin, a Yankee Doodle far from dandy.

1. "Georgie the port-controller, undignified in straw [a rustic hat?], disgraces himself, no buts about it."

2. "[A] woman caws like a crow." In response to the hat, one supposes.

3. "Where there is hatred of buoys [i.e., of the British colonial administration, clearly marking the line separating the safe channel of the established order from the danger-filled surrounding chaos], whoever so chooses has pounded [crushed, bruised, ground] everything to bits, and Georgie the port-controller reigns. How about that!"

Tu marques et tu marques et
  Tu bâilles, effet typique.[1]
Heaume et gaine! Heaume et gaine!
  Gigoté chic![2]
Tu marques et tu marques et
  Tu bâilles, effet tac.[3]
Heaume et gaine! Heaume et gaine!
  Gigoté Jacques.

1. "You mark and you mark and you yawn, a typical effect." The speaker is evidently chiding, rather scornfully, an individual engaged in marking or writing something, perhaps a small merchant marking prices on merchandise for sale or totting up his take.

2. "[My] helmet and sheath! [bis] [My] fine prancer!" (Gigoté: a horse strong in the hind legs.) It appears that the speaker is a horseman, very possibly a wandering knight, who longs for action, though the fact that both the items of military gear he apostrophizes are protective in function suggests that he is not really all that keen for a fight, the true purpose of his crying out being, one suspects, to proclaim his moral superiority, as a warrior, over his money-grubbing interlocutor. Incidentally, his steed is named Jacques (see last line).

3. When the persistent marker yawns a second time the speaker notices a clicking sound (tac). While the first known mention of dentures occurs in a manuscript of the year 1728 by the French dental surgeon Pierre Fouchard, it is conceivable that Fouchard's compatriot the persistent marker, an enterprising person clearly endowed with singleness of purpose, could centuries earlier have devised for himself a set of artificial teeth, which, by permitting him to smile broadly, would have made it easier for him to ingratiate himself with customers.

· 3 ·

Ivre folle d'où orle doit s'appelle paille[1]
Ane dol des six voisines que[2]
En dol détruit sueur braie d'Anchise[3]
Ouate! Coup d'hui doux fort, trine que[4]

The manuscript page bearing these verses is torn along the right-hand edge, and the monosyllabic verbs at the ends of lines two and four are missing. Even so, it is clear what the poet is up to: he recounts old gossip about a disreputable woman of antiquity — a witch or a wayward goddess — until, in sudden disgust, he renounces the theme.

1. "Drunken madwoman from where [an] orle must be called straw." An orle is either the fillet under the ovolo of the capital of a column or a narrow band bordering a shield without touching its edges; its function in both architecture and heraldry is ornamental. Calling an orle straw (i.e., denigrating it) signifies, then, showing contempt for mere display.

2. "Donkey fraud of six neighbor women that . . ." Did the felonious *folle* sell her ass to each of half a dozen women and then decamp on it? If so, who was maddest then?

3. "In [the] fraud, Anchises's sweat pants [were] destroyed." Given the nature of the destroyed garment, it is reasonable to assume that Anchises is not here the aged king who was borne from burning Troy by his son Aeneas but the same individual in his athletic youth, when his beauty was such that Venus fell in love with him. This in turn raises the intriguing possibility that Venus and the drunken madwoman are one, which would account for the latter's relieving Anchises, by fraud or otherwise, of his breeches.

4. "Rubbish! A sweet, strong drink right now, trine that . . ." Sick of his tale, the poet wants to lave his tonsils with a swig of wine. "Trine" may here be an astrological term denoting a favorable positioning of two planets, but without the final verb one cannot be certain.

Tuie-nickel, tuie-nickel, lit tel se tare.[1]
Ah! Ouaille ou âne d'ère ouate, Io art.[2]
Apais-boeuf[3] d'où Eure lasso Aÿ[4]
Laïque Adda immonde[5] y ne Daces caille.[6]

This fragment of what appears to be a treatise on husbandry modeled on Vergil's *Georgics* opens on a practical note but quickly slips into mythological, zoological, geographical, and ornithological confusion.

1. "A bed made of brushwood and nickel deteriorates."

2. "Io [in Greek myth the daughter of Inachus, king of Argos, of whom Zeus became enamored] was skilled at making quilts from contemporary sheep or donkeys."

3. An *apais-boeuf* must logically be an appeaser or pacifier of oxen (cf. *pique-boeuf,* an ox-team driver or goadsman), but since an ox has undergone "the most unkindest cut of all" (Shakespeare) that creature can hardly be a heifer, such as the one Zeus turned Io into when his wife Hera became jealous. So *addio, Io.*

4. "From where the Eure lassoes [ensnares] Aÿ." But the Eure does no such thing, since Aÿ (pop. 4,700; see 13) is on another tributary of the Seine altogether, the Marne.

5. "The secular, filthy Adda." More dubious comment, in this case offensive to local sensibilities, anent another perfectly respectable tributary. The Adda rises, in fact, nowhere in France but in the Rhaetian Alps of northern Italy, flowing southwest into Lake Como, then south to the Po, which it enters near Cremona.

6. "There [on the Adda] there are no Dacian quail" (Dacia: modern Romania). As an exasperated Italian reader might exclaim, *Basta!*

Pise, pas riche, hâte,
Pise, pas riche, colle,
Pise, pas riche, y n'appâte.[1]
Naine désole.[2]
Sceau malachite[3] hâte,
Sceau malachite colle,
Sceau malachite y n'appâte,
Naine désole.

1. "Not rich, Pisa hastens, cleaves to, and fails to lure." Having fallen to Florence in 1406, in the Guelph-Ghibelline wars, proud Pisa has lost her wealth. The city fathers hastily appeal to their allies, but for want of money to use as bait cannot attract their aid.

2. "The female dwarf devastates [ravages, lays waste]." To make matters worse, the plague or some other scourge cuts the Pisans down (to size).

3. The "malachite seal" of the second and repetitive quatrain (malachite: a green mineral carbonate of copper used for ornamental stonewear) presumably stands for Pisa's government.

Isar reine[1] y Nice peau-riz ne.[2]
D'ioule manie sonore (Hine).[3]
   Y Ouen tube aide?[4]
   Oui, d'accole. Denis aide.[5]
Indique où daine gaie toupie ne morne (Hine).[6]

A rather broad interpretation seems in order here.

1. Isabeau de Bavière (1371–1435), queen of France (born in Munich, on the river Isar).

2. She does not, after the fashion of Nice, use rice powder.

3. She has, however, a mania for sonorous yodeling, brought on by cognac. (Hine is a well-known brand.)

4. Will Saint Owen (609–683, bishop of Rouen) help her with his ointment in a tube?

5. Yes, he will put them together. Saint Denis (third century, first bishop of Paris) will also help.

6. If, however, indications are that the dear thing (*daine:* doe), instead of being gay as a spinning top, is sad, she should resort to her usual tipple.

O âne fort témoigné,
Tous forts dés chauds,
Tris tous gais de redits,
Ane fort — tous gaus.

This jingle can be readily Englished as:

O thou, proven strong ass,
All strong hot dice,
Odd tricks with gossip gay,
Strong ass — all lice.

It is presumably a piece of scurrilous satire in verse, like the so-called Mother Goose rhymes that have long been popular in England. The "strong ass" is probably a foolish king given to gaming and gossip, but which? the description would fit any of several French monarchs. Incidentally, while admiring the poet's brilliantly compressed characterization of the courtiers as *tris* (literally odd tricks, as in whist or bridge), we must suppress the temptation to assign twentieth-century meanings to *âne* and *gai*, although a derogatory comment on the licentiousness of the court may in fact be intended. Anyway, the poet's low opinion of king and courtiers, as summed up in his last word, needs no elucidation.

Très bel aï n' de maïs
Si à Oudh héronne.[1]
Des Halles Roi Naphte de phare mer soif[2]
Chicot taffetas tel suite de carvi naïf.[3]
Didier voyou[4] si sachée saille t'ignore l'aï
Fesse[5] très bel aï n' de maïs.

In these symbol-cluttered lines the unknown poet seems to be making portentous statements the precise meanings of which remain out of reach, conceivably because they were supposed to be understood only by initiates, perhaps fellow members of a secret society. The poet's knowledge of his world is impressively broad: thus the opening lines suggest a familiarity with natural history and geography, the next line (though less certainly) with commerce and economics, the next again with botany, and the next with history.

1. "A very handsome three-toed sloth, not of maize, if the female heron [flies] to Oudh." Both the sloth and maize (U.S., corn) are indigenous to South America; Oudh is a region of north central India now in the state of Uttar Pradesh. (For more on cultivation in South America see 34.)

2. "From Les Halles, King Petroleum of the lighthouse, sea thirst." Les Halles is, of course, the wholesale food market that until recently occupied a large site in the center of Paris; though *naphte* now means "naphtha" it formerly meant "petroleum." Startlingly, the line seems to deal with the shipping of crude oil by sea. (See 19.)

3. "Such a taffeta-covered stump following after an artless caraway plant." In the poet's view the man derisively called King Petroleum, probably a royal official, is a foppish but intractable (stumplike) individual very different from his naïve and easily swayed (plantlike) predecessor.

4. "Hooligan Didier." Since the two Didiers remembered in French history were, respectively, the last king of the Lombards, dethroned at Pavia by Charlemagne in 774, and a bishop of Langres martyred in the third

century and later canonized, the poet's characterization of him as a hooligan (guttersnipe, street urchin) implies a vehement antipathy to the state or the church or both.

5. "If the sackful juts out you know nothing of the sloth buttock . . ." The hooligan king's or bishop's "sackful" *may* refer to the contents of his codpiece, erect in anticipation of his sodomizing the good-looking sloth, but if it does, the naughty monarch/prelate is, the poet assures us, not to realize his vile intention.

• 9 •

Arques! Arques![1] Des docks doux, barques.[2]
Bégayeurs commis (ne tous Taoans[3]).
Samoane rague, samoanes dagues,
Indo-ananas, vélo-vite gaoan.[4]

1. This is clearly neither the commune of Arques in the Pas-de-Calais (pop. 7,200; glassmaking, jute-working, papermaking) nor the market town of Arques in the Seine-Maritime (pop. 2,740; artificial silk), where Henri IV defeated the duc de Mayenne in 1589, but the coastal river of the name, which forms the harbor of Dieppe.

2. "From the sweet docks, ships." "Sweet" apparently alludes to the aromas of the Oriental cargoes — spices, etc. — being off-loaded.

3. "Stuttering clerks (not all Taoists)." To the parochial Dieppois, the Chinese ship's clerks, tallying the cargoes aloud in their clipped vernacular, sound as if they are stuttering. Taoists are followers of the teachings of Lao-Tse (sixth century B.C.).

4. Cargoes include Samoan hemp for making rope (which chafes), Samoan daggers, Indian pineapples, and a high-speed bicycle from Gao, on the Niger River in West Africa. (Gao, once the capital of the Songhai Empire, is now a city (pop. 12,000) in Mali.)

Salut, mon grandi,
Borgne, non mandé.[1]
Crie ce nom tout-cité,
Marie, dont «ouais» ne se dit.[2]
Tu qui l'entoures se tais,
Ourson ferrailles dit:[3]
D'ail dans sainteté,
Beurrée dans santé.[4]
Décesse diane
D'oeufs sales, O mon grandi.[5]

1. "Hail, my grown one, one-eyed and not sent for." The speaker is evidently addressing a youth, perhaps his son, whose monocularity has kept him from being summoned to priestly service.

2. "Shout that name on everyone's lips, Mary, of whom *ouais* is not said." *Ouais* (what! my word!) appropriately expresses wonder but is too slangy to be used in referring to the Mother of God.

3. "Thou who encloseth it [Mary's name] in thy heart art silent, while the little bear [heretical—i.e., non-Mariolatrous—Russia?] speaks of it with irony [*ferraille:* scrap iron]," to wit:

4. "Garlic [evil-smelling] in saintliness, bread and butter [fattening] in health."

5. "So ends the reveille of bad eggs, O my grown one." High time too, one feels.

Beau-bis Chauffe-tôt[1] se gante, houe, scie,
Sille (vers bâclés) sonne, Nice nie.[2]
Iles combat (Cannes-mer, Rémy).
   Banni, Beau-bis Chauffe-tôt.[3]

Beau-bis Chauffe-tôt braille étain-fer,
Comminue d'août Nice.[4] Y'est l'eau![5] Ere
Ismaïlienne.[6] Faux rêve air-mer.[7]
   Banni, Beau-bis Chauffe-tôt.[8]

1. The identity of this romantic personage — Twice-Handsome Soon-
Heated — is obscure, but cf. Philippe le Bel and Harry Hotspur for
analogues. He would appear to be a Provençal Paul Bunyan, a folk hero.

2. Evidently an archetypal cultivator and builder, he "pulls on his gloves,
he hoes and he saws; he intones a Greek satire (with slipshod verses) and
he repudiates Nice."

3. Following this last act of hubris fighting breaks out between the
nearby towns of Cannes and Saint-Rémy, and the hero is banished.

4. Outraged, he "bawls aloud [in tones of] tin and iron" and in August
reduces Nice to powder (*comminuer:* to pulverize), only to discover

5. that Nice (like Cannes) is on the sea! This leads to

6. the Ismailian Era, or heyday of the Riviera. (Ismailis, members of a
sect of the Shiite branch of Islam, are followers of the Aga Khan, and for
several generations successive Agas, fabulously wealthy playboys, set the
pace for the smart international set that congregated on France's Côte
d'Azur in pursuit of pleasure. Hence the name.)

7. But the dream of a sea- and salt-air paradise proves false, and

8. Twice-Handsome Soon-Heated is again banished.

Coucou doux de Ledoux,
Madame a ce lot, cet air chou.[1]
Mais masse terce, l'eau se tisse, fidels instiguent . . .[2]
Anneaux se nattent ouateux d'houx.[3]

A sad and all-too-familiar tale of marital infelicity, quickly told.

1. "Sweet cuckoo of Ledoux . . ." Mme. Ledoux, her husband's "sweet cuckoo," possesses a certain attribute: an endearing air.

2. But she puts on weight (by a third!) and simultaneously dries up, whereupon the faithful lovers turn on one another, inciting quarrels.

3. "The wedding rings are plaited in a woolly mass—of holly." A brilliantly effective oxymoron!

Aÿ a délit tel note tri:
  Noces sans cul de dite ber.¹
Botte asile fait notr' mec
  Inde-Gaule (d'Aisne), père
De qui.² Neuf spahis nocent d'haute terre
  Qui aiment tout vice et demi:³
Aine-dols, faux redits secs,
  Oeuvres malignes—tels notent tris.⁴

Plus ça change . . . Readers of French newspapers will be unsurprised that the venue of these squalid goings-on is not the wicked capital but a placid provincial town: Aÿ (pop. 4,700) on the river Marne.

1. "Aÿ has an offense that needs sorting out: the unconsummated nuptials of a so-called launching cradle," evidently an unmarried young woman about to give birth.

2. "The [unborn infant's] father, a Franco-Indian fellow born in the Aisne, takes refuge in flight" (*Botte asile:* boot refuge; cf. the expression used of refugees from tyrannous regimes, "to vote with one's feet").

3. Nine Algerian troopers who "love all vice and a half"—i.e., and then some—descend "from high ground to go on a spree."

4. Their spree gives rise to "misrepresentations of groins [inflated codpieces?], gossip both false and dry and 'malignant works,'" all of which plainly call for sorting out in their turn.

· 14 ·

Qu'on me laisse. Tôt bête,
Cécile y piète,
Tarée ouaille. Le sais, salaud!¹
Putain, z'y pote
C'est ce gredin Goth.
Oui, elle sape effort; oui, gau.²

The spontaneous outpouring of a heart lacerated by jealousy, these lines
are addressed to a comrade who has apparently been so tactless as to
mention the poet's former sweetheart.

1. "Let me be. That stupid Cecilia is being stubborn, the damaged sheep.
I know all about it, you dirty dog!"

2. "Whore that she is, she's keeping company with that rascally Goth.
Yes, you louse, yes; she does sap my strength."

Rabais dab dab
Trille, ménine, taupe.[1]
Hindou d'yeux tines, que débit?[2]
Débouchoir du bécarre
De canne d'élastique maigre.[3]
Trop d'émaux, nefs alterés.[4]

Of all the rhymes in the manuscript this one is surely the most puzzling. To be sure, the commercial note of *rabais* is echoed by *débit;* but what has this to do with the references to music and musical notation, viz., *trille* and *bécarre?* Is a contrast intended between the almost blind mole and the Hindu with watercask eyes? And what exactly is *canne d'élas-tique maigre?* (See 21.) In the circumstances, the best course may be to give a literal translation of the verses in the hope that some reader steeped in sixteenth-century French symbology will succeed in unlocking their meaning.

1. "Rebate [price reduction, discount] father father/ Trill, noblewoman companion of a royal princess, mole."

2. "Hindu with watercask eyes [a great weeper?], what debit [sale, shop]?"

3. "Uncorker of the natural note/Of cane [reed, walking stick, rod] of thin elastic."

4. "Too many enamels, naves [ships] changed for the worse [tampered with]."

A Die,[1] le radeau-lare,
Etienne aux claques scolaires,
Ou à Thème Aix, yucca méso-Saône?[2]
Youyou, c'est tout, comme
A Tène aux claques.[3]
Bâte naos; yucca mat, none.[4]

This fragment consists of a question put to one *"Etienne aux claques scolaires"* (Stephen of the school claques) and his reply. Stephen is evidently a wandering scholar who hires out as a paid clapper at lectures. He is questioned as to the whereabouts of a certain raft, which is dubbed, presumably in jest, a lar—i.e., a tutelary god or spirit of the ancient Romans.

1. Die (pop. 3,900), on the river Drôme, is the site of Gallo-Roman remains, which may account for the raft's being called a lar. The Drôme rises in the Alps and empties into the Rhône.

2. Is the raft-lar at Die "Or at the Aix Topic, the yucca in mid-Saône?" The river Saône, another tributary of the Rhône, rises in the Vosges and flows south to enter the Rhône at Lyon. The appearance on an island in that river of yucca—a chiefly tropical New World plant—would certainly excite the interest of naturalists, and the fact that the phenomenon is called the Aix Topic suggests that it has occurred earlier at or near Aix-les-Bains, on the east bank of Lake Bourget.

3. Instead of answering the question directly, Stephen replies that the raft-lar is simply "A dinghy, that's all, like [the one used for] the claques at Tène." La Tène, at the eastern end of Lake Neuchâtel in adjacent Switzerland, is an ancient Celtic site that has given its name to the cultures of the late Iron Age. The La Tène culture is characterized by an art style that drew upon Greek, Etruscan, and Scythian motifs and translated them into highly abstract designs in metal, pottery, and wood.

4. "Load up the naos; dull or lifeless yucca, the nones." Stephen's terse closing remarks bespeak an acquaintance with classical architecture (the

naos is the central interior part of a Greek temple, between the pronaos and the opisthodomos). His final words seem to indicate that his next lecture will be on the yucca (presently not in flower) at 3 P.M. (Nones, the fifth of the seven canonical hours, designate the ninth hour after sunrise, ordinarily reckoned as about 3 P.M.)

<h1 style="text-align:center">· 17 ·</h1>

Fille . . . faille . . . faux . . . femme . . .
Aïe![1] Semelle de blaude évanouie (ne glisse manne).[2]
Bée y à l'ail-vore, bée y d'aide.[3]
A la graille[4] (ne dis ce beaune tout)[5] Mecque, maille, brette.[6]

1. "Daughter . . . faille . . . imitation [fabrics] . . . wife . . . Ouch!" The speaker is pained by his womenfolk's preoccupation with clothes.

2. "Underside of a blouse that's vanished (not slipping into the hamper)." A typically banal family crisis.

3. "Here gaping at the garlic-eater, there her helper all agape." The women's mute overreaction to the trivial loss provokes the speaker to sarcasm. Incidentally, he may also find his wife's addiction to garlic provoking.

4. "In the manner of the crow," or "As the crow flies."

5. "Don't say it's all [on account of] this Beaune" (a Burgundy wine). The speaker's muddled syntax suggests, however, that he has in fact had one or two glasses too many.

6. "Mecca, chain mail, long sword." The speaker longs to abandon his family and go off on a Crusade to end Crusades, straight to the enemy's capital. By implication, he asks, "Wouldn't you, in my place?"

Signe, garçon. Neuf Sikhs se pansent.
   Epoque aide fous, lève railles.[1]
Faure Antoine, tes blagues bercent,
   Bec dine à paille.[2]

Ouenza paille oiseau peine
   De berce bécane. (Tu signes.)[3]
Oie sonate date, édentés dix
   (Tous sept): biffure de quine.[4]

De qui noircit Nice, caouane de noces,
   Caouane de notice manie?[5]
De cuits noirs cygnes, deux par l'heure,
   Y tine braie d'Annonay.[6]

Deux mai, dois signe de gare d'Aisne.[7]
   Anne guigne août d'écluse.
Ouen d'août ne qu'aime à blague Berthe.
   Anne se nippe tôt, faire noce.[8]

If the second and third of these stanzas present difficulties for the modern reader, they probably made perfectly good sense to sixteenth-century Picards. On the other hand they may easily be nonsense; if so, the fact is readily accounted for by their source, as the poem is put in the mouth of a professional fool or jester. He is addressing a boy, one Antoine (Anthony) Faure, whom he has chosen to be his apprentice and presented with indenture papers for his, the boy's, signature.

1. "Sign, boy. Nine Sikhs are bandaging themselves." (The notion of Hindu devotees wrapping their heads in turbans doesn't seem hilarious today, but in the sixteenth century, when Sikhism was founded, it was at

least novel.) "The times help fools and promote mockery" — i.e., the outlook is promising for a career in folly.

2. "Anthony Faure, your humbug sends people to sleep, [your] mouth dines on straw." In the fool's opinion young Anthony could profit from professional instruction.

3. "Ouenza straw bird punishment of hogweed bicycle. (You sign.)" Hogwash — but see above; anyway, the boy signs up. (Ouenza is a mountainous region of Algeria close to Tunisia.)

4. "Goose sonata date, the toothless ten (all seven): crossing-out of a *quine*" (i.e., the series of five winning numbers in a lottery). Three mysterious numbers — 10, 7, 5 — in just one and a half short lines! The picture of ungainly geese performing an elegant musical composition has a certain piquancy. While geese have no teeth, the "toothless ones" are masculine and therefore cannot be geese (though in a pinch they could be ganders); whoever or whatever they are — and whether there are ten or seven of them — they apparently cancel out the luck of lottery winners.

5. "From whom blackened Nice, tortoise of weddings, tortoise of a mania for accounts?" Clearly the fool is not addressing his protégé here. Can the tortoise he apostrophizes with talk of "blackened Nice" possibly be Beau-bis Chauffe-tôt (q.v., 11), the legendary destroyer of that city?

6. "Of cooked black swans, two per hour, there watercask breeches of Annonay." These birds must be allegorical, since the first true black swans were not discovered until the nineteenth century, in Australia. Annonay, pop. 12,600, in the Ardèche, is a center of both papermaking and silk culture, suggesting that the tub-size trousers may be made from one of these materials.

7. "The second of May, you must sign from the Aisne station." This *gare*, obviously not a railway station, is probably a siding or dock on a river or canal. The fool seems to have forgotten that the boy has already signed the papers. In specifying the date he is, in effect, saying that the time for fun and games — May Day, the first, yesterday — is over, and that one should now get down to the serious business of folly.

8. To round out his monologue the fool recounts a tale of low romance in August featuring a singularly dreary trio: Anne, given to ogling or leering at a canal lock; Owen, who "doesn't enjoy teasing Bertha"; and the shadowy Bertha. Presumably by turning her well-practiced leer on Owen, the first-named girl apparently beats out her rival for his affections, for in the last line "Anne soon buys a trousseau to make a wedding."

Roc à bail, bey bis;
On détruit tape.[1]
Où N. de Windt blouse,
Décret de l'huile roque.[2]

Ouais, ne débarbe rex,
Décret de l'huile fol.[3]
Inde août, Noël comme crételle,
Bey bis indol.[4]

In the light of the present world situation with respect to oil, this little tale has a startlingly contemporary ring, though the oil in these verses was presumably of another kind altogether, e.g., olive or palm. The story's central figure is a swarthy (grayish-brown or brownish-gray) Near Eastern official — a bey — and the others a European king and a certain N. de Windt, presumably a Dutch or Flemish political leader, probably republican.

1. The bey is informed that there is a rook or castle (as in chess) to let, the defenses of which have been destroyed. (A small European country he can buy up at will?)

2. Where de Windt cheats (on paying for imported oil?) he is checked by the oil decree — evidently a law laid down by the oil producers, including the bey. The oil decree is said to "castle" (roquer) — a defensive move in chess in which the king and a rook are placed on opposite sides of one another.

3. For his part, the king is not unbored (an ironic understatement) by the "crazy" oil decree, no respecter of monarchy.

4. The bey, sitting pretty, enjoys an indigo August (i.e., a cool blue one) and a Christmas sufficiently green and mild to be likened to a kind of grass. He ends up smelling of roses (indole is a white crystalline compound obtained from coal tar that is used in making perfume).

Goussets, goussets, Gandhara,
Ouï-dire châles à oindre.[1]
Houppes tercent, danses tercent,
Indignes mélodies chambrent.[2]
Dérailles mettent anneaux de Man
Ou Oudh, nattent saïs prières.[3]
Atout qui me baille de lève-lac
Intrus y me donne de stères.[4]

1. "Armpits [*bis*] of Gandhara [a historic region of northwest India, now in Pakistan], rumor has it that shawls are to be rubbed with oil." To mask the body odors inevitably encountered in hot places?

2. "Pompons and dances now cost a third more than they used to and indecent tunes keep a body from leaving his room." In other words, the old values — of the marketplace and of public morality — are crumbling.

3. Fortunately, these lapses (literally, derailments) give rise to salutary developments: (a) they "put on the rings of Man or Oudh" (reaffirm the dominance of Celtic culture, characterized by the working of precious metals in exquisite jewelry, from Oudh (in India, near Gandhara) in the east to the Isle of Man in the west) and (b) they "plait together [in an effective whole] the prayers of pious syces" (stablemen or grooms, especially in India; i.e., ordinary, honest folk uncorrupted by trends like the one toward indecent tunes).

4. The poet sums up in a metaphor the reflection that unwelcome innovations can bring benefits. The same blow, he writes, that foists on him an intrusive (unwanted) "lake-raiser" (i.e., a dam, creating a reservoir behind it) provides him with abundant fuel (*stère:* a cubic meter, usually of firewood) for poetic protest.

Jacques abbé Nîmes-able,[1]
Jacques bec couic,[2]
Jacques, j'aime pas voir
Ta canne d'élastique.[3]

These lines might be translated as:

James, priest convertible,
Bird of bright chaff,
James, I don't like to see
Your rubber staff.

1. *Nîmes-able:* susceptible of being converted to Protestantism. Throughout the sixteenth-century civil wars over religion, Nîmes (chief town of the Gard) was an important Huguenot stronghold.

2. *Bec couic:* beak chirp. In two syllables Father James is characterized unforgettably as birdlike in appearance and given, like a bird, to incessant chattering.

3. The priest-abbot's staff symbolizes his religious faith, and the poet is, as a good Catholic, dismayed by its evident elasticity. (NOTE: A female acquaintance points out that since several women poets were active in France in the middle years of the sixteenth century—e.g., Louise Labé, "La Belle Cordière," c. 1520–1566—the author of these lines may have been a woman, in which case Father James's "elastic staff" could conceivably refer to something less abstract and even more private than his faith.)

Dindons bels
Peu saisis Noël.¹
Où peut terrine?
Lille (Jean égrène).²
Où poule déroute?
Lille (Tom masse cet août).³
Ouate à noter bouille, oies se datent,
Tout droit une pour pousser quatre,
Où Nevers didyme aînée arme.⁴
Anne qui le dit maïs anise fadeur se borne.⁵

These lines are about the preparing of food in northern and east central France, but since we know nothing of the peasants mentioned or their cooking methods, much is unclear. The reader may wish to attempt his own reconstruction from the literal linear translations given below.

1. "[This] Christmas there is little demand for fine turkeys."

2. "Where can the pot [be]? At Lille, where John is shelling [peas into it]."

3. "Where [did] the hen go astray? At Lille, where Tom is working hard this August."

4. "Noteworthy wadding boils [and] geese date themselves, one bolt upright in order to push four, where didymous [two-part, twinned] Nevers [chief town of the Nièvre] arms the-firstborn girl."

5. "Anne [the armed firstborn *Nivernaise?*], who says it [i.e., who is the source of the foregoing information], limits herself to flavoring the flat-tasting corn [maize] with aniseed." Licorice corn! (For a report on an equally bizarre flavoring practice followed by another cook farther south, see 32.)

Héroïque Garonne de moule-bourrée bouche,[1]
Moule-bourrée bouche, moule-bourrée bouche.
Héroïque Garonne de moule-bourrée bouche,
    On accole daines féroces, tes maures naines.[2]

Dix-six douées, oui, oies sarcleuses,[3]
Oies sarcleuses, oies sarcleuses.
Dix-six douées, oui, oies sarcleuses,
    On accole daines féroces, tes maures naines.

Dix-six douées, huit collines à Rome,[4]
Collines à Rome, collines à Rome.
Dix-six douées, huit collines à Rome,
    On accole daines féroces, tes maures naines.

These verses chronicle the arrival by sea, in southwest France, of some diminutive Moorish ladies, possibly making up the harem of a visiting Arab or Berber dignitary, who, being models of submissiveness, are jocularly called "ferocious does." They arrive unannounced, but a gaggle of sixteen clever geese warns of their approach — just as, in 390 B.C. in Rome, the cackling of sacred geese awoke the defenders of the Capitoline Hill in time to repel a sneak attack by invading Gauls. *These* visitors, however, are made welcome.

1. "Heroic Garonne of the mussel-filled mouth." There is nothing especially heroic about the Garonne, which rises in the Pyrenees, but in combination with talk of mussels the characterization is obviously not meant to be taken literally; the tone of these lines is, indeed, clearly *mock-heroic*. Before chemical plants and refineries arose in Bordeaux, moreover, mussels were abundant around the river's mouth, at the head of the Gironde estuary.

2. "We embrace the 'ferocious does,' your petite Moors [literally, dwarfs]."

3. "Sixteen gifted ones, yes, weeding [grazing] geese." Note the old-style cardinal number: a modern poet would write *seize*.

4. "Sixteen gifted ones, eight hills at Rome." The poet is in error about the number of hills on which Rome was built—actually, of course, not eight but seven.

· 24 ·

Scie à peine,[1] Anne pique étape
Halle de Dés,[2] ioule ave (goût de lac).[3]
Scie à peine, Anne lit vite lais,
Ioule ave (bas de lac), Halle de Dés.[4]

1. The ubiquitous Anne, who turns up yet again in this quatrain, "saws hardly at all." If sawing wood is here a metaphor for sleeping, Anne has had little sleep.

2. She "pricks" (pops in at) an emporium known as the Market of Dice, so called, perhaps, to distinguish it from markets without a gambling concession.

3. There, she "warbles a Hail Mary in the manner of a lake," i.e., liquidly.

4. On another occasion, again after little sleep, Anne "quickly reads ballads, warbles a Hail Mary" (but less pleasingly this time, sounding like a lake *bottom*, which suggests a muddy delivery) and again goes shopping.

Lille bouée bel-U comble-eaux hier orne.[1]
De chippes scène de méd-eaux,[2] de caoua scène des cornes,[3]
Où hérisse de bouée, où luxe have terre de chippes?[4]
Y sondera Estaque, faste aise lippe.[5]
Huile, yeux, ouais! qui me nonante taille.[6]
(Forêt faille d'houx, île chère, Lys craille.)[7]

1. "Lille sound buoy U once adorned [the surface at] high water." Lille (pop. 191,900) in French Flanders, lies on the river Deûle.

2. These "scraps of cloth in mid-river" are presumably discarded ends from the city's textile plants (cotton and linen).

3. "Coffee at the scene of the horns" may refer to the morning-after consumption of *café-au-lait* by adulterous lovers. (A cuckolded husband is said to wear horns.)

4. "Where does the buoy pop up, where does luxury undermine the land of scraps [Lille]?"

5. The first question is answered directly: the buoy "will sound [the waters off] L'Estaque," an industrial suburb of Marseilles. But the second question is answered obliquely, with the assertion that "ostentation eases the outthrust lower lip," that is, the pout: by flaunting their wealth, the owners of Lille's textile plants will not undermine the workers' morale but lessen their resentment.

6. In an abrupt shift the poet excitedly announces the discovery of oil, a gusher he estimates to rise "ninety [*pieds,* or feet] high."

7. This leads to anxious reflections anent the oil strike's possible harmful effects on the surrounding region: the "forest garlanded with holly" and the "beloved city" of Lille. Downstream, the river Lys, into which the Deûle empties, will "caw like a raven"—that is, cry out in protest against the pollution.

Crie, ce mât cis-Comines;
Dégoût cesse, gâtine fat.[1]
Plisse, tu peux taper néant:
D'ioule Manès hâte.[2]
Fieu à veine gâte-à-penné,
A Epernay huile d'houx.[3]
Fieu à veine gâte-à-Epernay,
D'Aisne godent blé, chou.[4]

This octave recalls the long struggle (thirteenth and fourteenth centuries) for possession of Flanders between the Leliaerts (supporters of the French king, so named for the fleur-de-lis on the French arms) and the Clauwaerts (supporters of the count of Flanders, so named for the lion's claws in the count's shield). In his opening quatrain the poet, a staunch Leliaert, exhorts his hearers to rally around the fleur-de-lis.

1. "Cry up this (flag)pole this side of Comines; let the disgust [arising from this] morass of conceit be no more." Comines (Flemish Komen) on the river Lys, straddles the Franco-Belgian border.

2. "[Even] folded, you [the fleur-de-lis standard] can strike out at nothingness: the hasty yodelings of Manichaeism" (personified by Manes, the third-century Persian prophet who propounded that syncretic dualistic religious philosophy). This imputing of heresy to the enemy is an early instance of the use of the Big Lie in psychological warfare.

3. "Lucky young fellow, bird-spoiler [penné: pinnate, feathered or winged, and the young man is presumably handy at killing birds] holly oil to Epernay" (pop. 21,400, on the river Marne, champagne).

4. "Lucky young fellow, Epernay-spoiler, the wheat and cabbage of the Aisne [region] become rumpled." How the fortunate youth could have spoiled or despoiled Epernay with holly oil is a mystery.

Bâille, bébé; bonne tine.
(Dadais se connaît en tines.)[1]
Tu guèdes un lit tel, rhabites squine.[2]
(Tour apaise bébé, bonne Tinéenne.)[3]

This charming ditty is addressed to a baby, with parenthetical asides to a grown-up.

1. "Yawn, baby; have a nice tub. (The booby knows a thing or two about tubs.)"

2. "You wet such a bed and again inhabit China root"—i.e., become overexcited. China root, or ginseng, is a well-known excitant.

3. "Going for a stroll pacifies both the baby and the good woman of the Tinée," evidently its nurse. (The Tinée, a river of the Alpes-Maritimes, flows south some seventy-two kilometers to join the Var.)

Docteur Fausse-terre[1]
Huée ne tout glossateur[2]
(Enna, Chaouïa, Varennes).[3]
Y se tait, petit n'a pas d'elle,
Raille tape, touille smille dol.[4]
"Ah, neveux, houez ne terre Reggane."[5]

1. "Doctor False-ground," appears from what follows to be a philosopher given to arguing from doubtful premises.

2. He prudently does not jeer at every interpreter or commentator.

3. That these centers of learning (and glossing) are located in, respectively, Sicily, Morocco, and northeastern France shows that his fame is widespread.

4. But the diminutive (*petit*) philosopher is very human: for lack of a female companion (*n'a pas d'elle*) he "falls silent, mocks failure, and stirs up a spalling hammer fraud," doubtless letting the chips fall where they may.

5. "Ah, nephews," he says, "hoe not the soil of Reggane"—a warning about unreliable farmland from, of all people, Doctor False-ground! But here, notably, the philosopher does not live up (or down) to his name or sobriquet: the logic of his pronouncement is unassailable, as Reggane is located in the Algerian Sahara, a region quite unsuited to cultivation. The recipients of this piece of avuncular advice must have found it puzzlingly self-evident. On the other hand, the learned doctor may have simply been passing along to them his conviction, the bitter fruit of long experience, that, like tilling the desert, trying to cultivate the minds of blockheads is a pointless enterprise that can never produce anything of value.

Lit de la polie féline dresse,
Ça témoigne, dessine darse,
Ou hors mine apprête élite delt' Ouse.[1]
Or, mâts d'arquais manquent hauteur;[2]
Rince pinque de Renaud T. d'eau-terre;[3]
Force Pau et lignards, nasse noue close.[4]

Notwithstanding the innocent-sounding allusion at the outset to an "elegant cat" — presumably a powerful political figure who is to be laid in his grave — these lines clearly outline a proposed naval/military expedition against Pau in southwestern France, in which certain English noblemen will participate as volunteers. Every line but the fourth is couched in the imperative mood.

1. The person addressed is instructed to "Make the elegant cat's bed, bear witness to same, sketch a harbor or, outside a mine, prepare the leading citizens of the Ouse delta." Which Ouse delta is meant is unclear, as there are three English rivers of that name: one empties into the English Channel and another into the Humber, while the third comes out (like so much else) in The Wash.

2. "Now, masts of the Arques [on the Channel; see 9] lack [sufficient] height."

3. "[Therefore] rinse Reginald T.'s ship from water-earth," i.e., free her from the mud in which she is stuck and wash her down. A *pinque* is a narrow-sterned sailing ship of the Mediterranean, in English a pink or pinkie; the positive identification of Renaud T. awaits further scholarship.

4. "Take Pau and its foot soldier defenders, [and so] tie up and close [the] lobster pot [or rat trap]." It is hard to see what role a ship could fill in this operation other than transporting the English volunteers, etc. to southwest France, inasmuch as Pau is almost 300 kilometers inland from the Mediterranean and 100 from the Atlantic.

Dit delà, dit de la dame pleine, maçonne Jeanne.[1]
Ohé! ne tout bédouin de stock Hai-nan.[2]
Oie ne choux offre à nuance chouane.[3]
Dit delà, dit de la dame pleine, maçonne Jeanne.

1. The poet announces the "far-out story" (*dit delà*) of the "solid lady" Joan, who, most unusually for one of her sex, is a mason or bricklayer.

2. "How now! [She's] not just any old Bedouin with a stock of Chinese goods." "Bedouin" seems to mean here an itinerant peddler; Hainan, a large island in the South China Sea off the Chinese mainland, would be a logical supply source for merchants trading with the Far East.

3. "The goose does not offer cabbages [more likely tempting cream buns, *choux à la crème*] to the Chouan shade [or hue]." The Chouans were insurgent Breton royalists who in 1793 were to rise against the central republican authority, and *nuance* implies a tendency toward or sympathy with a cause rather than all-out espousal of it, so the sense seems to be that the goose (Joan?) has no truck with Chouan sympathizers. Incidentally, the frequency with which geese turn up in these poems suggests rather forcefully a link — even, conceivably, a common source — with the contemporaneous folk tales that Charles Perrault collected in a famous book he published in 1697 subtitled *Contes de Ma Mère l'Oye*, "Tales of Mother Goose."

Trille ouaille semaine:[1] neuf goddams
(Des huées ne tous)[2] scient inné bol.[3]
Endives de bol-là débinent ces tronqueurs,[4]
Maille sans guède bine l'engoueur.[5]

1. "Sheep trill week," week when the sheep trills; i.e., a topsy-turvy week when anything can happen.

2. "Nine Englishmen (not all hooting)." A very French view of the English as sacrilegious barbarians is implicit in these words, the source of the French *goddam* — Englishman — plainly being the foreigners' penchant for taking the Lord's name in vain.

3. The intruders saw in bits — i.e., cut up with a toothed blade — the "innate bowl," presumably a cherished artifact, a vicious act of vandalism. However,

4. "endives in the bowl disparage these mutilators" — by making them ill? — and

5. "chain mail without woad harrows the obstructor," i.e., armed Frenchmen, pointedly not painting their bodies blue with woad in the manner of ancient Britons, avenge the Englishmen's act of desecration by giving them what for, thus turning the tables on them for a truly topsy-turvy dénouement.

Halte élue est-ce Thoré: [1]
Oeufs, chacun nourri
A noeud,[2] mais c'est tort: est-c'épigone?[3]
Haltère lieu à nadir:
Oeufs Jacques, anise-brodeur![4]
A nous mystère y se donne.[5]

1. "Thoré is a chosen stopping place." The Thoré is actually a river in the Massif Central that flows into the Agout, so the reference must be to its valley — in particular, as the text makes clear, to a certain inn in that valley.

2. Every egg served there is "nourished to the knot" — i.e., packed with nutrients.

3. "But there is [something] wrong" with them: are they prepared by an inferior chef? (The Greek *Epigonoi* — from the plural of *epigonos*, born after — were sons of the Seven against Thebes who imitated their fathers by attacking Thebes; hence an epigone is a second-rate imitator or follower.)

4. "The dumbbell place [i.e., the inn, so called because its manager acted stupidly in allowing the egg crisis to develop] at its nadir: eggs in the manner of Jacques the aniseed-exaggerator!" The recipe in question calls for excessive amounts of licorice-flavored aniseed; no wonder the eggs taste peculiar!

5. Thus "the mystery there yields itself up to us."

Dès roi sage au lit (mi-lourd ou onces)
Livres donne, dérive vers dits.[1]
Y où orque danse cinq fera mornes thona-ites.[2]
Nul arc maure, bel ail d'anille.[3]
Ah! ne dis ce debout! redonne avis oncques:
Fou rêveur joue, se toupille.[4]
Aïe! Carrefour néo-bidet, nonne à taille.[5]
Ah! cénobitiques erses fourmillent.[6]

1. Since the wise king [took] to [his] bed ... he hands out books [or money; *livres* could mean either] and derives spoken verses," presumably rhymed addresses of thanks. The poet's parenthetical characterization of the royal philanthropist as "semi-heavy or ounces" suggests that he considers him a lightweight.

2. "Where the killer whale dances five [i.e., thrashes about at a tempo faster than 4/4 time] he will make tuna-fanciers unhappy"—no doubt by decimating the tuna. The king is apparently subject to murderous fits.

3. "No Moorish arch, fine garlic of tendril." The Moorish arch symbolizes stability, but the unstable king is more like a flexible shoot.

4. "Ah! don't say he's on his feet! [Well, then,] sound again [the] warning, [as] ever: the crazy dreamer is at play, he's spinning himself around like a top." The king is evidently undergoing one of his seizures.

5. "Oh! [interjection denoting a twinge of pain] the new bidet crossroads, [a] tall nun." Since *bidet* originally meant a pony, nag, or small horse, *néo-bidet* must mean that innovation, the bathroom fixture one straddles to wash the genitals. Is the tall nun shopping for one at the crossroads?

6. "Ah! Gaelic-speaking monastic types are milling about." If the tall nun *is* shopping for a bidet, she could well find the presence of these Irish and/or Scottish monks painful; but what have they and she to do with the king?

Litre dérape savoir-terre:[1]
Littorale graine, ça verse Andes.[2]
Mais qui démaille thé, aux chiennes![3]
Andes plaie, sainte lande.[4]

Here we have a ringing indictment of an abuse of sound land management perpetrated, allegedly, by the settlers who came after the conquistadors in New Spain.

1. "A liter tears out earth-knowledge," i.e., wine drinking blots out awareness of basic facts of agronomy, in particular that

2. "a seed planted on the [Pacific] coastal plain overturns the Andes."

3. "But whoever undoes [sows] tea, to the dogs with him!" (literally and emphatically, to the "bitches").

4. "Andes wound, holy barren." The area thus devastated becomes hallowed ground.

NOTE: While the Spanish colonial planters were guilty of appalling crimes against the indigenous peoples of New Spain, it is unlikely that they ever attempted to grow tea, a plant that requires ample rainfall, on the mostly arid Pacific littoral of South America. By "tea" the poet may, of course, have meant *cannabis sativa*, the drug derived from which, marijuana, could indeed persuade a person who took enough of it that the nearby mountains were falling down. If so, however, his indignation seems a bit excessive—another instance of French xenophobia (see 31)—considering that that plant, used in China to induce euphoria from very early times, had been known and grown in Europe, including France, since A.D. 500 or even earlier.

Lie de l'atome tocard,
Cygne fort — Esope ère.[1]
Ouate Chalais-ite:
Ouaille,[2] de Bréda ne batteur.[3]
Ah! hou! Chalais cote tête?[4]
Oui-da! Où terre, naïf?[5]
Ah! hou! Chalais marri.
Oui, doute erre:[6] ouaille F.[7]

We can state with near certainty that these lines deal with an actual historical event, one that occurred in 1626; they could therefore only have been written that year or subsequently. But by 1626 several decades had elapsed since the bulk of the verses in the manuscript were putatively composed, i.e., the middle or late sixteenth century, so we have to assume that this poem was a later addition. It is about Henri de Talleyrand, marquis de Chalais (1599–1626). A favorite of Louis XIII, Chalais was accused of conspiring against Cardinal Richelieu, and beheaded.

1. "Lees of the worthless atom, strong swan — [it recalls] Aesop's time." With characters like an atom (King Louis, so called to indicate that he is next to nothing) and a swan (Richelieu, who dominates the king), this tale could have been spun by the great fabulist himself.

2. "The Chalais standard [literally, wadding]: a fleece [literally, a sheep] ..." This fleece is almost certainly intended to remind the educated reader of Jason's Argonautic expedition in quest of the Golden Fleece. Jason is thus identified with Chalais, the Argonauts with his fellow conspirators, and the Golden Fleece with the conspirators' goal of freeing the king (who has not yet shown himself to be worthless) from Richelieu's domination.

3. "[The fleece's] beater [i.e., maintainer, curator] not from 'Breda.'" The Breda quarter of Paris was formerly the home of the *demi-monde;* hence

these words convey, in a coy and roundabout manner, the information that Chalais is of noble birth.

4. "Ah! Boo! Doesn't Chalais value [literally, assess] his head?"

5. "Yes, indeed! Where [on] earth [is the] innocent?"

6. "Ah! Boo! Chalais is sad [sorry, aggrieved]. Yes, there is no doubt of it [literally, doubt wanders off, departs]."

7. His fleece is marked F—for *Fin* (French) or *Finis* (Latin).

· 36 ·

Nids de lassantes pignes, nids de lassantes pignes.[1]
Où aîné mène merise, y ce trop-bleu subit guigne.[2]

A rustic jingle for children containing two "improving" messages anent the local flora.

1. "Nests of tiresome pine cones" (*bis*). This seemingly nonsensical phrase establishes the scene as a region of conifers (in Champagne? the Ardennes?) and encourages a grown-up indifference toward the pine cones many children like to play with.

2. "Wherever an eldest son takes wild cherries, that overly inexperienced one undergoes bad luck"; i.e., don't eat wild fruits or you may have a stomachache. [In French, curiously, a greenhorn can be either green (e.g., *la verte jeunesse:* callow youth) or blue (e.g., *un bleu:* a tyro, novice, or rookie).]

Ecotée, picotée, maille blague qu'est-ne,[1]
Chez les aigues fors gênes telles mène —[2]
Gênes telles mène comme Eve ridée![3]
Tôt Siouah démaille blague qu'est-ne d'hôtelier.[4]
Ça me taille m' Sinaï nonne, ça me taille ma soutane.[5]
Ecotée, picotée, maille blague qu'est-ne.

A nun in far-off Egypt testifies as to how she got the habit.

1. "Chain mail, stripped down and pierced with tiny holes, mocks what is not": i.e., military men, being realists, scorn airy imaginings.

2. "[It] brings such embarrassments before the water tribunals," courts at which the reality or unreality of a given proposition is established by its upholder's undergoing the well-known trial by water.

3. One such embarrassment is the concept, clearly heretical, of a "wrinkled Eve," Eve with wrinkles!

4. In short order Siwa (an Egyptian oasis, pop. 5,200, and apparently the site of a water tribunal) undoes this fabrication, the tall story of an innkeeper (who presumably perished by drowning in defending it).

5. "This converts [shapes, carves] me into a nun of the Sinai, this fits me out in my soutane" — a garment she apparently regards as a guarantor of truth, her own form of chain mail. (It would seem that the soutane or cassock, now worn by Roman Catholic priests, was once also worn by members of some religious orders.)

Hâte, carrosse bonzes.
Hâte, carrosse bonzes.[1]
Oie n'est pennée, tu à peine, eh?[2]
Hâte, carrosse bonzes.

Ah, tu caresses bonnes!
Ah, tu caresses bonnes![3]
Fieu à veine, tes nuits douteuses
    Guillent; va, dames touiller, resonne![4]

The setting of this pleasing song about the hard days and joyous nights of a rickshaw boy is obviously Far Eastern. Dating it presents a problem, since France did not impose its rule on Indochina until after 1867. We must assume, then, that it is the work of a very early settler in Saigon or some other city of the region — an unusually observant and compassionate merchant, perhaps, or even an exceptionally broadminded missionary.

1. "Hurry, convey Buddhist priests in a carriage."

2. "The goose isn't feathered and you hardly are either, isn't it so?" The rickshaw boy's lack of feathers means that he is poor (cf., to feather one's nest) and must work for his living. Can the featherless goose symbolize Indochina, a region the first European visitors likened to the fabled goose that laid golden eggs, but that is already perceived to be, in reality, no such thing?

3. "Ah, you caress maids!"

4. "You lucky young rascal, your dubious nights positively ferment" — like so much beer; "go stir the women up and ring for them again!"

· 39 ·

Tuie de la dame Anne, tuie de lady
    Egarée (tôt faillite? ébats d'elle?)[1]
Forte houille de la dame cède tuie de lady.
    Ah! de ce poêle dizaine aïs, six nus ratels.[2]

Geste d'haine, filou bâille.[3] Emonde cet escroc,
    As bellacquaise hétaire, Beryl![4]
Ouiche! ferraille-étain, bottes de héros. Sots![5]
    Dey Koweït fagote, d'air quoi, réel.[6]

NOTE: the use of *tuie* (scrub, brushwood) to denote the lady Anne's estate suggests that the estate lies in southwestern France, where *tuie* means *ajonc*, furze or gorse. And since the region, Aquitaine, was under English rule until 1451, the lady may be English.

1. The scene is set: the "gorse-covered lands of the lady Anne," who is distraught (*égarée*), either because of impending bankruptcy (*tôt faillite*) or as a consequence of her frolics and revels (*ébats*).

2. The lady's property yields lots of coal (*forte houille*). Out of her coal mine (poetically called a *poêle*, or stove) troop exotic animals making up an underground menagerie: "some ten three-toed sloths [and] six unclothed honey badgers."

3. Enter, yawning hatefully, a swindler (*filou*), ostensibly male.

4. Recognizing the newcomer, the poet cries, "Cut down that crook, the ace adventuress from Bellac, Beryl!" (Bellac, pop. 5,100, in the Haute-Vienne, is a center of tanning.)

5. "Fat chance! 'Heroes' [hereabouts have] feet of lead [literally, boots of old iron and tin]. Dolts!" The Picard poet pointedly disparages Gascon claims (cf. *The Three Musketeers*) to superior courage.

6. Coolly, the dey of Kuwait, who has evidently used Beryl as an *agente provocateuse*, ties up (*fagote*) the valuable real estate (*réel*).

Oui, oui, les huit ne-quis, ranz taureau de Thônes.[1]
Opposent se taire, sondant cet air (sinistres nattes goanes).[2]
Rapinade d'ouïe en dos, craillants trous de loques.[3]
Art d'Achille de Rennes aligne Bade, fort noise, état cloque.[4]

The setting of these lines is the vicinity of Thônes (pop. 3,000) in the Haute-Savoie. Even in that Alpine Eden, it seems, there are human serpents ready to turn it into a hell.

1. Eight "nobodies" (literally, not-whos) are singing the *ranz taureau* of Thônes — and perhaps also tooting on their alpenhorns, in which case the din must be horrendous. The *ranz taureau* (bull *ranz*), all memory of which has disappeared, was probably a pastoral melody similar to the well-known *ranz des vaches* of neighboring Switzerland.

2. The revelers decline to pipe down, instead ringing changes on the *ranz* and in so doing producing noises the poet likens to baleful mats from the Portuguese colony of Goa, in India. Conceivably the poet is comparing the interweaving aural patterns of the song with the unpleasant or disturbing patterns visible on the mats.

3. Apparently not satisfied that the foregoing image is sufficiently forceful or clear, the poet has another go at it, describing the hideous cacophony as "a backward piece of bad painting to the ear, cawing holes in rags."

4. Here the poet reveals himself to be a staunch partisan of law and order, expressing the hope that Achille (Achilles) de Rennes, evidently a puissant local personage, will line up Baden — that is, call in mercenaries from that German city — to restore public tranquillity, if need be by force, since, as he observes, with "great quarreling, the state blisters." (NOTE: as *cloquer* has another quite different meaning, the poet may have meant to say that the state "breaks wind" — an apt metaphor, in any case, for an abrupt loss of prestige or "face.")

Afterword

Although the Coucy Castle *rames* had sounded tantalizingly familiar from my first reading of them in manuscript form, it wasn't until this book was in galleys that I finally found out what made them so. I was, for the umptieth time, going over the lines that begin "*Salut, mon grandi*" when I suddenly "heard" the words of the English nursery rhyme "Solomon Grundy." Stunned, I turned to other *rames;* each promptly conjured up another familiar ditty. What a shock! Far from the fresh and sprightly verses I had taken them to be, the *rames* were merely sterile constructions, the end products of a dilettantish game in which their author(s) had aimed at nothing more than mimicking in French the sound of English verses!

This discovery was, to say the least, upsetting. It meant, of course, that my labors to explicate the *rames* had been a complete waste of time. If the book were published, I would be exposed as a scholarly fool and my publisher as an ignorant and gullible accessory.

At my desk, where I had first glimpsed photostats of the old French verses three years before, I reached for the telephone to call my editor, but something stayed my hand; instead, I flipped through my encyclopedia to the entry on nursery rhymes. To my astonishment I read that almost no nursery rhyme could be dated to before 1600. Feeling, all at once, quite giddy, I rushed out to my local public library and there confirmed the happy fact.

Having been compiled in the 1500s, the *rames* couldn't possibly be imitations of English nursery rhymes, since these didn't yet exist. On the contrary, they were indisputably original compositions.

But if the English rhymes hadn't inspired the French *rames*, the French must have inspired the English, so close and consistent was the phonetic correspondence between them. This could have happened, I realized, during the years before the Edict of Nantes (1598) ended France's religious wars. Protestant Picard émigrés in London would surely have congregated in taverns, and when they did, what could have been more natural than that they should have recited or even sung their native *rames?* Local taverngoers, hearing the verses as French-accented English, might well have been captivated by their directness and simplicity, learned them by heart, and little by little made them their own. And as the French rhymes became a part of English oral tradition, they would have been forgotten in France, the usual fate of such ephemera.

Students wishing to compare the *N'Heures Souris Rames* with the nursery rhymes to which they apparently gave rise will find the latter on the following pages.

O. DE K.
July 4, 1980

· 1 ·

Georgie-Porgie, pudding and pie,
Kissed the girls and made them cry;
When the boys came out to play,
Georgie-Porgie ran away.

· 2 ·

To market, to market,
  To buy a fat pig.
Home again, home again,
  Jiggety-jig.
To market, to market,
  To buy a fat hog.
Home again, home again,
  Jiggety-jog.

· 3 ·

If all the world was apple pie
And all the sea was ink,
And all the trees were bread and cheese,
What could we do for drink?

· 4 ·

Twinkle, twinkle, little star!
How I wonder what you are,
Up above the world so high
Like a diamond in the sky.

Pease porridge hot,
Pease porridge cold,
Pease porridge in a pot
Nine days old.
Some like it hot,
Some like it cold,
Some like it in a pot
Nine days old.

It's raining, it's pouring,
The old man is snoring.
  He went to bed
  With a cold in his head
And he couldn't get up in the morning.

One for the money,
Two for the show,
Three to get ready,
And four to go.

Three blind mice,
  See how they run.
They all ran after the farmer's wife;
She cut off their tails with a carving knife.
Did ever you see such a sight in your life
  As three blind mice?

Hark, hark, the dogs do bark,
Beggars are coming to town;
Some in rags and some in tags
And one in a velvet gown.

Solomon Grundy,
Born on a Monday,
Christened on Tuesday,
Married on Wednesday,
Took ill on Thursday,
Worse on Friday,
Died on Saturday,
Buried on Sunday.
This is the end
of Solomon Grundy.

Bobby Shaftoe's gone to sea,
Silver buckles on his knee;
He'll come back and marry me,
  Bonny Bobby Shaftoe.

Bobby Shaftoe's bright and fair,
Combing down his yellow hair,
He's my ain for evermair,
  Bonny Bobby Shaftoe.

Cock a doodle doo,
My dame has lost her shoe;
My master's lost his fiddling stick
And knows not what to do.

I had a little nut tree,
  Nothing could it bear
But a silver nutmeg
  And a golden pear.
The King of Spain's daughter
  Came to visit me
And all for the sake
  Of my little nut tree.

· 14 ·

Come, let's to bed,
Says Sleepyhead;
Tarry a while, says Slow;
Put on the pot,
Says Greedy-gut,
We'll sup before we go.

· 15 ·

Rub-a-dub-dub,
Three men in a tub,
And who do you think they be?
The butcher, the baker,
The candlestick maker;
Throw them out, knaves all three!

· 16 ·

A diller, a dollar,
A ten o'clock scholar,
What makes you come so soon?
You used to come
At ten o'clock,
But now you come at noon.

· 17 ·

Fee, fie, foh, fum,
I smell the blood of an Englishman.
Be he alive or be he dead
I'll grind his bones to make my bread.

· 18 ·

Sing a song of sixpence,
A pocket full of rye;
Four and twenty blackbirds
Baked in a pie.

When the pie was opened
The birds began to sing;
Was not that a dainty dish
To set before the king?

The king was in his counting house,
Counting out his money;
The queen was in the parlor
Eating bread and honey.

The maid was in the garden
Hanging out the clothes,
When down came a blackbird
And snipped off her nose.

· 19 ·

Rock-a-bye baby
On the treetop,
When the wind blows
The cradle will rock;

When the bow breaks
The cradle will fall
And down will come cradle,
Baby and all.

· 20 ·

Goosey, goosey, gander,
Whither shall I wander?
Upstairs and downstairs
And in my lady's chamber.
There I met an old man
Who would not say his prayers;
I took him by the left leg
And threw him down the stairs.

· 21 ·

Jack be nimble,
Jack be quick,
Jack jump over
The candlestick.

Ding dong bell,
Pussy's in the well.
Who put her in?
Little Johnny Green.
Who pulled her out?
Little Tommy Stout.
What a naughty boy was that
To drown poor pussycat,
Who never did him any harm
And killed the mice in his father's barn.

Here we go round the mulberry bush,
The mulberry bush, the mulberry bush;
Here we go round the mulberry bush
On a cold and frosty morning.

This is the way we wash our clothes,
Wash our clothes, wash our clothes;
This is the way we wash our clothes
On a cold and frosty morning.

This is the way we clean our rooms,
Clean our rooms, clean our rooms;
This is the way we clean our rooms
On a cold and frosty morning.

See a pin and pick it up,
All the day you'll have good luck.
See a pin and leave it lay,
You'll have bad luck all the day.

Little boy blue, come blow your horn.
The sheep's in the meadow, the cow's in the corn.
Where is the boy who looks after the sheep?
He's under a haystack, fast asleep.
Will you wake him? No, not I,
For if I do, he'll surely cry.

Christmas is coming,
    The goose is getting fat,
Please to put a penny
    In the old man's hat.
If you haven't got a penny
    A ha'penny will do;
If you haven't got a ha'penny,
    Then God bless you!

Bye, baby bunting,
Daddy's gone a-hunting
To get a little rabbit skin
To wrap his baby bunting in.

Doctor Foster
Went to Gloucester
In a shower of rain.
He stepped in a puddle
Right up to his middle
And never went there again.

Little Polly Flinders
Sat among the cinders
Warming her pretty little toes;
    Her mother came and caught her
    And spanked her naughty daughter
For spoiling her nice new clothes.

Diddle, diddle, dumpling, my son John
Went to bed with his stockings on;
One shoe off and one shoe on,
Diddle, diddle, dumpling, my son John.

Three wise men of Gotham
They went to sea in a bowl,
And if the bowl had been stronger
My song had been longer.

· 32 ·

I'll tell you a story
Of Jack a Nory,
And now my story's begun.
I'll tell you another
Of Jack and his brother.
And now my story is done.

· 33 ·

There was a jolly miller once
    Lived on the River Dee;
He worked and sang from morn till night,
    No lark more blithe than he.
And this the burden of his song
    Forever used to be,
I care for nobody, no, not I,
    As nobody cares for me.

· 34 ·

Little drops of water,
    Little grains of sand,
Make the mighty ocean
    And the pleasant land.

· 35 ·

Little Tom Tucker
Sings for his supper;
What shall he eat?
White bread and butter.
How shall he cut it
Without e'er a knife?
How shall he marry
Without e'er a wife?

· 36 ·

Needles and pins, needles and pins,
When a man marries his troubles begin.

· 37 ·

Hickety, pickety, my black hen,
She lays eggs for gentlemen;
Gentlemen come every day
To see what my black hen doth lay.
Sometimes nine and sometimes ten,
Hickety, pickety, my black hen.

· 38 ·

Hot cross buns,
Hot cross buns.
One a penny, two a penny,
Hot cross buns.

Hot cross buns,
Hot cross buns.
If you haven't any daughters
Give them to your sons.

· 39 ·

Tweedledum and Tweedledee
    Agreed to fight a battle,
For Tweedledum said Tweedledee
    Had spoiled his nice new rattle.

Just then flew by a monstrous crow
    As black as a tar barrel,
Which frightened both the heroes so
    They quite forgot their quarrel.

· 40 ·

Wee Willie Winkie runs through the town,
Upstairs and downstairs, in his nightgown,
Rapping at the windows, crying through the lock,
Are the children all in bed? for now it's eight o'clock.

Bibliography

American Heritage Dictionary. New York: American Heritage Publishing Co./Houghton Mifflin, 1969, 1970.

Baring-Gould, William S. and Ceil. *The Annotated Mother Goose.* New York: Bramhall House, 1962.

de Cossé-Brissac, Philippe. *Châteaux de France Disparus.* Editions "Tel," 1947.

de Kay, Ormonde. *Rimes de la Mère Oie.* Boston: Little, Brown, 1971.

Harrap's Standard French and English Dictionary, Part One: French-English, with Supplement (1962). London: George G. Harrap & Co., 1968.

Lefèvre-Pontalis, E., *Le Château de Coucy.* Paris: Henri Laurens, *éditeur*, 1909.

Opie, Peter and Iona, eds. *The Oxford Nursery Rhyme Book.* Oxford: Oxford University Press, 1955.

Petit Larousse. Paris: Librairie Larousse, 1967.

The New Columbia Encyclopedia. New York: Columbia University Press, 1975.

van Rooten, Luis d'Antin, *Mots d'Heures: Gousses, Rames.* New York: Viking, 1967.

Index

N'Heures Souris Rames
The Coucy Castle Manuscript

was designed by Katy Homans
typeset by A & S Graphics
and printed by the Book Press